ENDANGERED
ANIMALS OF THE
NORTHERN CONTINENTS

Barbara J. Behm
Jean-Christophe Balouet

For a free color catalog describing Gareth Stevens' list of high-quality books, call 1-800-542-2595 (USA) or 1-800-461-9120 (Canada). Gareth Stevens' Fax: (414) 225-0377.

The editor would like to extend special thanks to Jan W. Rafert, Curator of Primates and Small Mammals, Milwaukee County Zoo, Milwaukee, Wisconsin, for his kind and professional help with the information in this book.

Library of Congress Cataloging-in-Publication Data

Behm, Barbara J., 1952-
    Endangered animals of the northern continents/Barbara J. Behm, Jean-Christophe Balouet.
        p. cm. -- (In peril)
    "Adapted from Ces espèces qui disparaissent . . . with original text by Jean-Christophe Balouet"--T.p. verso.
    Includes bibliographical references (p. 30) and index.
    ISBN 0-8368-1079-1
    1. Endangered species--Europe--Juvenile literature. 2. Endangered species--Asia--Juvenile literature. 3. Endangered species--North America--Juvenile literature. [1. Endangered species.] I. Balouet, Jean-Christophe. Ces espèces qui disparaissent. II. Title. III. Series: Behm, Barbara J., 1952- In peril.
    QL83.B44   1994
    591.52'9'091813--dc20

                                                            94-11675

This edition first published in 1994 by
Gareth Stevens Publishing
1555 North RiverCenter Drive, Suite 201
Milwaukee, Wisconsin 53212, USA

This edition © 1994 by Gareth Stevens, Inc. Adapted from *Ces Espèces qui Disparaissent,* © 1990 by Editions Ouest-France, with original text by Jean-Christophe Balouet. This edition published by arrangement with David Bateman, Ltd. Additional end matter © 1994 by Gareth Stevens, Inc.

Picture Credits
André Aaron (with the courtesy of the Mammals and Birds Laboratory of the National Museum of Natural History of Paris): pp. 18 (lower), 25; British Museum: pp. 22, 23, 27; Jacana: Cover, pp. 6, 8, 12, 13 (both), 14, 16, 18 (upper and middle), 19, 20, 21, 26; National Library: pp. 9, 11, 17; Central Library Museum, National Museum of Natural History of Paris: p. 10; Planet pictures: p. 28; Vincennes Zoo: p. 15

Series logo artwork: Tom Redman

Series editor: Patricia Lantier-Sampon
Series designer: Karen Knutson
Research assistants: Diane Laska, Derek Smith
Translated from the French by: Anne-Marie Jardon-Sampont
Map art: Donna Genzmer Schenström, University of Wisconsin-Milwaukee Cartographic
    Services Laboratory

Printed in the United States of America

1 2 3 4 5 6 7 8 9 99 98 97 96 95 94

At this time, Gareth Stevens, Inc., does not use 100 percent recycled paper, although the paper used in our books does contain about 30 percent recycled fiber. This decision was made after a careful study of current recycling procedures revealed their dubious environmental benefits. We will continue to explore recycling options.

INTRODUCTION

For millions of years, during the course of evolution, hundreds of plant and animal species have appeared on Earth, multiplied, and then, for a variety of reasons, vanished. We all know of animals today — such as the elephant and the rhinoceros, the mountain gorilla and the orangutan — that face extinction because of irresponsible human activity or changes in environmental conditions. Amazingly, hundreds of species of insects and plants become extinct before we can even classify them. Fortunately, in modern times, we are beginning to understand that all living things are connected. When we destroy a plant species, we may be depriving the world of an amazing cure for human diseases. And we know that if we destroy the forest, the desert creeps forward and the climate changes, wild animals die off because they cannot survive the harsh conditions, and humans, too, face starvation and death. Let us remember that every creature and plant is part of a web of life, each perfect, each contributing to the whole. It is up to each of us to end the destruction of our natural world before it becomes too late. Future generations will find it hard to forgive us if we fail to act. No matter what our age or where we live, it is time for every one of us to get involved.

Dr. Jane Goodall, Ethologist

CONTENTS

Words that appear in the glossary are printed in **boldface** type the first time they occur in the text.

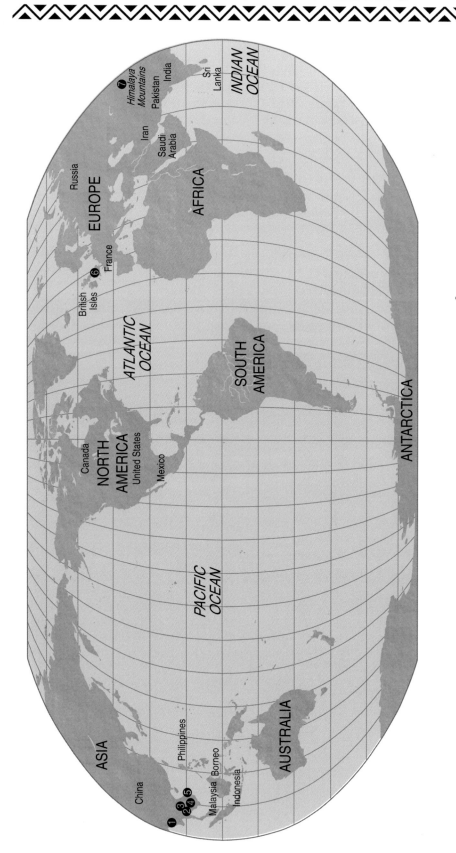

MAP KEY:
1. Myanmar (Burma)
2. Thailand
3. Laos
4. Cambodia
5. Vietnam
6. England
7. Tibet

▲ For various reasons, many species of plant and animal life on Earth are in great peril of disappearing forever. Unfortunately, this danger is not limited to any one place; it has become a global problem. From the northern and southern continents to the islands in Earth's oceans and seas, a long list of irreplaceable animal species needs the help and protection that only human resources can now provide. This map indicates some of the specific continents, countries, bodies of water, and other world areas referred to in *In Peril: Endangered Animals of the Northern Continents.*

BETWEEN YESTERDAY AND TOMORROW

Centuries of agriculture and cattle raising have transformed the lands of western Eurasia. Since humans first settled the area, many species of wildlife have become **endangered**. Many animals have fallen victim to the destruction of their **habitat** as well as to hunting, pollution, and **pesticide** poisoning.

Forests cover much of the eastern areas of Eurasia. But human overpopulation and the logging industry destroy these valuable forests on a daily basis. The forests provide homes for hundreds of animal **species** that seem destined for **extinction** in the near future.

Regions of northern Asia are home to many types of wildlife, including the brown bear, lynx, wolf, sable, ermine, and various species of birds. There are fewer people living in the northern and western parts of Asia than in other parts of the world, but hunting has still taken its toll on wildlife. In eastern and southeastern Asia, most wildlife, except for some species of birds, snakes, lizards, and crocodiles, have disappeared with human settlement of the land.

AMPHIBIANS AND REPTILES

Many Eurasian amphibians and reptiles are at great risk of disappearing forever. For example, the loggerhead turtle, *Caretta caretta*, and the Algerian or Iberian tortoise, *Testudo graeca*, both from the area of the Mediterranean Sea; an Asian pond turtle from the family Emydidae, *Batagur baska*; the Komodo dragon, *Varanus komodoensis*, of Southeast Asia; and the olm, *Proteus anguinis*, a southern European salamander, are all endangered.

5

The Chinese alligator, *Alligator sinensis*, is probably the most endangered alligator today. Its population decreased considerably from 1950 to 1960, years when human demand for crocodile skins was great. Humans still hunt this alligator, despite strict laws that exist to protect it.

▲ The Chinese alligator lives in the upper Yangtze River valley.

▲ The nearly extinct crocodile of Siam sometimes **crossbreeds** with the Indo-Pacific crocodile on breeding farms.

The crocodile of Siam, *Crocodylus siamensis*, is almost extinct in the wild. Once common throughout Southeast Asia, the best hope for its survival is **captive breeding programs**.

Philippine crocodiles, *Crocodylus mindorensis*; false gavials, *Tomistoma schlegelii*; and Indian gavials, *Gavialis gangeticus,* are also endangered.

Endangered snakes include the Central Asian cobra, *Naja naja oxiana*, and the Latifi viper, *Vipera latifii*. These serpents are victims of hunting by humans and mongooses.

BIRDS

The Oriental black ibis, *Pseudibis davisoni*, is particularly rare. Its dense, tropical habitats in Cambodia, Thailand, Vietnam, and Laos are difficult for scientists to reach. This discourages attempts that might otherwise be made to help preserve this species. Past wars in this area have also taken their toll on these birds, since humans hunted them for food.

Chinese monal pheasants, *Lophophorus lhuysii*, are very rare. Humans still hunt these peaceful birds in spite of their fragile existence. The Chinese monal pheasants, which visit forests that grow at high altitudes, may disappear in the near future if the hunting is not stopped.

The helmeted hornbill, *Rhinoplax vigil*, is hunted for its flesh, feathers, and the bony helmet that gives the bird its unusual profile. Items made from this bird are sold around the world. This international trade, along with the large-scale **deforestation** of Malaysia, could eventually lead to the total destruction of the helmeted hornbill.

▲ Humans hunt the endangered monkey-eating eagle even in the reserves.

The Italian gray partridge, *Perdix perdix italica*, numbers only a few dozen. This partridge has been the victim of overhunting. Its habitat is also being destroyed by changing methods of farming, including the use of pesticides.

Cabot's tragopan, *Tragopan caboti*, is a horned pheasant that lives in the mountains of southeastern China. This tragopan is endangered in the wild, and England is the only place outside China to have specimens in **captivity**.

Monkey-eating eagles, *Pithecophaga jefferyi*, are powerful **birds of prey**. They live in the Philippines and hunt for prey in tropical forests. The eagles' wings are wide but short, and their tails are long. Farmers complain that these eagles eat their poultry. The farmers take revenge by killing some of them. This, together with the

▲ Cabot's tragopan is fighting to survive in the wild.

destruction of forests, has reduced the possibilities of survival for these eagles.

Chinese crested terns, *Sterna zimmermanni*, are the most threatened of all terns and may even be extinct. The last sighting was in 1937, but the terns may still survive on a few islands in Southeast Asia.

The black-necked crane, *Grus nigricollis*, is a **migratory** bird from the Tibetan plateaus of China. The natural environment of this bird makes scientific observation

▲ The Javanese wattled lapwing has not been observed for more than fifty years.

already be extinct. The last observation of this species dates back to 1939, one century after its discovery. The original habitat of the lapwing, a member of the plover family, included open zones and cultivated land on the Indonesian islands of Sumatra and Timor. Its disappearance is due mainly to overhunting by humans.

somewhat difficult, and the number of sightings is extremely low. Only five adults and one chick were observed in 1976 during an organized search for this species in the Ladakh district of northern India on the southern border of Tibet.

Javanese wattled lapwings, *Vanellus macropterus*, may

The hoki, *Crossoptilon mantchuricum*, is a brown-eared pheasant found in the mountains of northern China. This beautiful species has been in decline for several years, and the destruction of its forest home poses the greatest threat to its existence. Zoos contain many of these birds, and captive breeding programs may be able to save this species from extinction.

MAMMALS

Wolves have been killed in various parts of the world by

▲ The hoki is disappearing rapidly from Chinese forests.

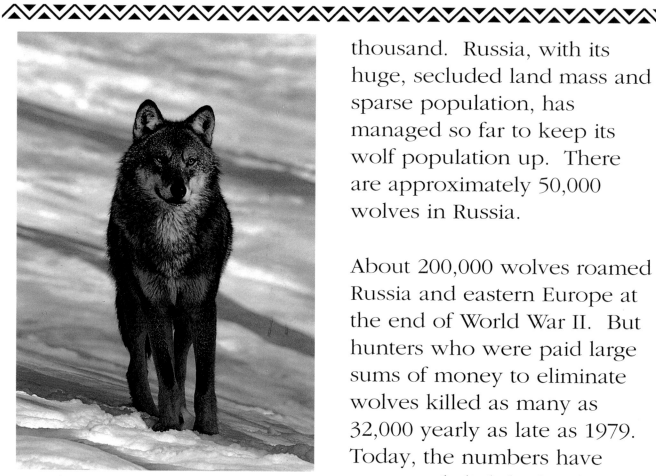

▲ Wolves are hunted worldwide.

thousand. Russia, with its huge, secluded land mass and sparse population, has managed so far to keep its wolf population up. There are approximately 50,000 wolves in Russia.

About 200,000 wolves roamed Russia and eastern Europe at the end of World War II. But hunters who were paid large sums of money to eliminate wolves killed as many as 32,000 yearly as late as 1979. Today, the numbers have recovered slightly, but hunting continues to decrease the wolf population.

farmers who are convinced the wolves prey on their livestock and other farm animals. Because of this, only a few wolves exist in Europe outside of zoos. At the beginning of the twentieth century, there were hundreds of thousands of wolves worldwide. Now, the world numbers, with the exception of Russia, are only a few

With the exception of a few wandering wolves from eastern Europe, the wolf was virtually extinct in France by the early 1900s. It is now nearly extinct in northern Europe and the British Isles.

Indeed, the greatest threat to wolves has been hunting by

humans. In Mongolia, 10,000 wolves were massacred in 1976 alone. The trade of wolf skins is the principal reason they are hunted.

▲ Tigers are the largest and most powerful members of the cat family.

The tiger is one of the most endangered Asian animals. At one time, there were seven subspecies of tigers. But the Bali tiger, *Panthera tigris-balica*, disappeared around 1952. The Java tiger, *Panthera tigris sondaica*, is perhaps also extinct today. At one time, the Java tiger was very abundant on the island. Imported guns during World War II, however, armed many hunters who killed the tigers in great numbers for their fur. By 1955, the population of Java tigers was estimated at only twenty-five specimens, half of which were in a reserve. Today, no Java tigers survive in the reserves.

Lions live mostly in Africa now, although they used to be more widespread. A few Asiatic lions, *Panthera leo persica*, still live on the

▲ Lions, such as this rare Asiatic lion from India, used to thrive in several areas of the world. Lions now live mainly in Africa.

Kathiawar Peninsula of India. But apart from these, the lion survives only in Africa.

The snow leopard, *Panthera uncia*, is one of the most beautiful felines in the world. It lives in the Himalaya Mountains of southern Asia at altitudes between 13,120 and 16,400 feet (4,000 and 5,000 meters). It generally lives in couples or in family groups. Unfortunately, some humans hunt the snow leopard for its beautiful fur.

Fifteen hundred specimens of the Indian elephant of Sri Lanka, *Elephas maximus maximus*, remain today. This small elephant lives only in a few reserves, but the majority of the reserves may soon be cultivated. If this is the case, there will not be enough natural habitat on Sri Lanka to sustain a wild population of these elephants.

China's Yangtze River dolphin, *Lipotes vexillifer*, is the most threatened sea mammal on the planet. This dolphin is represented by only a few hundred specimens.

Fishing is a direct cause of death for half of these dolphins. Sometimes, the

▲ The snow leopard is hunted as far as the highest summits of the Himalayas.

▲ The giant panda lives in great risk of disappearing.

dolphins are caught by the ends of baited lines; others are suffocated in nets. In addition, boat propellers can cause fatal wounds. Industrial water pollution and explosives used in construction along the riverbanks also harm these dolphins.

The giant panda, *Ailuropoda melanoleuca*, is the emblem

of the **World Wildlife Fund** and the international symbol for endangered species. Its disappearance is almost inevitable in the near future. The giant panda numbers about one thousand, a relatively high number compared to other species presented in this book. But, in this particular case, these numbers are too low to be encouraging. Valuable skins, disappearing habitat, and difficulty breeding in captivity all work to endanger the lives of these beautiful and irreplaceable animals.

▲ The Asiatic wild ass, threatened by epidemics of horse plague, almost disappeared thirty years ago.

Giant pandas have thick black-and-white fur. They live in the dense bamboo and rhododendron forests that grow at high altitudes in western China. They exist mainly on a diet of bamboo, but they may also eat other types of plants or even small animals. Unfortunately, the giant pandas' forest habitat is dwindling. The pandas roam their threatened homes either alone or in small groups.

Giant pandas were discovered in 1869. The first birth in captivity took place at the Peking Zoo in 1963. Today, about eighty-five pandas can be found in world zoos, but their reproduction is so difficult and slow that breeding in captivity offers little hope for this species.

The Asiatic wild ass, *Equus hemionus khur*, of India is a small, wild donkey. It currently numbers only about

▲ Only a few dozen Javan rhinoceroses remain in the world.

two thousand. It lives in the desert areas near Pakistan.

The rhinoceros of Java, *Rhinoceros sondaicus,* is the rarest large mammal in the world. It was once abundant in China, Laos, Vietnam, and Malaysia. It became extinct around 1900 in India, around 1920 in Myanmar (Burma), and around 1930 in Sumatra. The Javan rhinoceros population of about fifty-five animals now lives only on the Ujung Kulon reserve. The last roaming animal in the wild was killed in 1934.

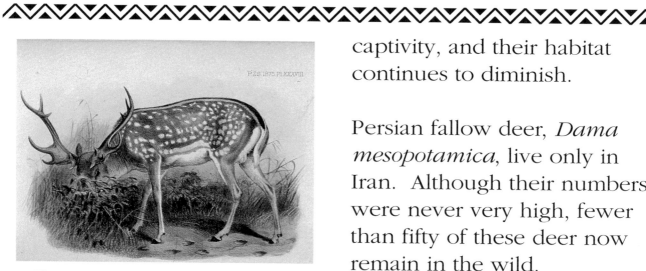

▲ There are only a few Persian fallow-deer in zoos and less than fifty in the wild.

captivity, and their habitat continues to diminish.

Persian fallow deer, *Dama mesopotamica*, live only in Iran. Although their numbers were never very high, fewer than fifty of these deer now remain in the wild.

Like all rhinoceroses, the Javan rhinoceros was hunted for its horn, which was supposed to have great medicinal value. This animal is still hunted, even on the Ujung Kulon reserve. No Javan rhinoceroses live in

▲ The Arabian oryx is often a victim of guns and motor vehicles.

▲ Eld's deer are nearly extinct in the wild.

Eld's deer, sometimes called the brow-antlered deer, makes its home in southern Asia. All three subspecies of *Cervus eldi* are in danger of disappearing forever.

Humans hunt the tamarau of the Philippines, *Anoa mindorensis*; the Tibetan yak, *Bos grunniens*; and the Arabian oryx, *Oryx leucoryx*. With the increasing number of automatic weapons and motor vehicles, there are few safe places for these animals in their natural environments.

The orangutan, *Pongo pygmaeus*, lives only in the tropical rain forests of Sumatra and Borneo. Logging poses the greatest threat to these animals. There are, at most, 4,000 to 5,000 orangutans left in the wild. Orangutans also run the risk of being captured for use as laboratory animals.

▲ The orangutan is a magnificent, but endangered, species.

DISAPPEARING WEALTH

North American wildlife was once abundant. Not too long ago, bison, bears, bighorn sheep, caribou, moose, puma, jaguars, and wolves roamed the continent freely.

The human population explosion in North America has greatly reduced the wildlife population. Farming has claimed much of the natural habitat, and logging continually destroys forests. Air and water pollution harm animals and their habitats, and humans continue to hunt dwindling wildlife species.

Caribou in North America have begun to disappear. The passenger pigeon, which once numbered millions of birds, is now extinct. The red wolf, the marmot, the whooping crane, the California condor, and many other species now are in terrible danger of extinction.

AMPHIBIANS AND REPTILES

The Houston toad, *Bufo houstonensis*; the leopard frog, *Rana pipiens fisheri*, of Nevada; the long-fingered salamander, *Ambystoma macrodactylum croceum*, of California; the narrow salamander, *Batrachoseps aridus*; the spotted salamander, *Ambystoma maculatum*; and the blind salamander, *Typhlomolge rathbuni*, of Texas are a few of the most endangered amphibians in North America. These species are dying mainly because of loss of habitat.

▲ Crocodiles are killed for their skins.

▲ Some snake species are nearly extinct because of habitat destruction.

Even in the deserts, reptiles are disappearing. The Mexican desert turtle, *Gopherus flavomarginatus*, is the most endangered turtle of the northern continents. The blunt-nosed lizard, *Gambelia silus*, of the San Joaquin River area, and the San Francisco garter snake, *Thamnophis sirtalis tetrataenia*, are also disappearing. Their habitats are being replaced by human development.

American crocodiles, *Crocodylus acutus*, are experiencing great losses.

Their skins are valuable to both leather dealers and their customers.

▲ The fate of the California condor is in the hands of humans.

Birds

The California condor, *Gymnogyps californianus*, is the best known endangered bird of prey of North America. This bird can reach a wingspan of about 10 feet (3 m) and a weight of 30 pounds (14 kilograms). Its numbers were no higher than forty birds in 1977. The condor is able to reproduce at five or six years of age, but only about 40 percent of the young reach the age when they can even leave the nest.

Condors seem to have been relatively abundant at the beginning of the century. But they became victims to poisoning, overhunting, and egg collecting. Because they eat the flesh of dead animals, many condors were poisoned by meat baits set by hunters.

The American whooping crane, *Grus americana*, is seriously endangered. It was never an abundant bird, with a population in 1860 estimated at 1,300 birds. The population located in Louisiana was forced from its migratory wetlands as farmers claimed the cranes' habitat for planting crops.

▲ The whooping crane, illustrated above by John James Audubon, has become very rare.

At about the same time, the whooping cranes of Texas, Iowa, Utah, New Jersey, Idaho, California, Illinois, and New Mexico in the U.S. and Manitoba, Alberta, and Saskatchewan in Canada progressively became extinct.

American researchers have created an **artificial population** of whooping cranes from eggs removed from nests. This species generally lays two eggs, but only one of the young is raised. So researchers have set about raising the young from the second egg. Today, the whooping crane population, estimated at two hundred in 1991, is increasing, and the species may be saved if the artificial population program can be carefully maintained.

The Clapper rail, *Rallus longirostris levipes*, is of Californian and Mexican origin. This bird visits salty, coastal swamps, where there is an abundance of a plant called glasswort. These swamps are becoming intensely polluted. They are also being drained for human development. The investment in land in these areas is extremely profitable. The approximately two hundred rails left will have a difficult struggle to survive.

The Eskimo curlew, *Numenius borealis*, is an endangered species that reproduces in the northern part of North America and **hibernates** in unknown regions of South America. Its populations were estimated at several million during the last century. No reproduction or hibernation site is known at present, and only a few curlews are sighted each year.

Eskimo curlews used to gather at the end of summer

▲ The Eskimo curlew is becoming more and more rare.

on the Labrador shores of eastern Canada before beginning their annual migration. But humans hunted great numbers of the birds on these shores in the 1870s and 1880s as the birds prepared to leave.

The ivory-billed woodpecker, *Campephilus principalis*, is a very large black-and-white bird. The male has a prominent red crest. This woodpecker, along with a subspecies, the imperial woodpecker, *Campephilus imperialis*, once occupied a large area in the southeastern United States and Cuba. The imperial woodpecker has not been observed for more than thirty years. The ivory-billed woodpecker is nearly extinct.

MAMMALS

Gray's bat, *Myotis grisescens*, lives only in the central and southeastern United States. More than 80 percent of its numbers were lost during the last twenty years. There are approximately 1.5 million specimens left, but these bats are particularly sensitive to human visits into their caves. If these bats happen to be disturbed, the entire **colony** will leave its shelter and never return. A single visit by humans into their cave, even if the visitors do not think humans are harmful, can have disastrous consequences for the bats.

Protecting Gray's bats is difficult because there seems to be no other suitable place than their original home to shelter them. It may seem that bats' underground habitats are safe from humans, but this is not true. Cave explorers in Virginia, for example, removed grates placed at the entrance of a cave to protect bats from human contact. Following the explorers' visit inside the cave, many bats mysteriously died.

▲ The Vancouver marmot may be a future victim of habitat destruction.

Vancouver marmots, *Marmota vancouverensis*, numbered only 230 animals in a 1984 survey. At present, loss of habitat is the worst threat to these marmots.

Prairie dogs, *Cynomys parvidens*, once lived in large numbers on the open plains of North America. One hundred thousand animals existed in the 1920s. But the prairie dog was nearly extinct by 1972. The estimated 6,500 animals left remain threatened because of the destruction of their natural territories for agricultural purposes.

The black-footed ferret, *Mustela nigripes*, still survives in low numbers in the central United States. In 1987, only eighteen of these ferrets were sighted. These eighteen were captured for a special breeding program, and, as of 1993, at least three hundred of these animals are in captivity.

▲ Humans hunt the black-footed ferret for its pelt.

Destruction of its prey, hunting by humans, and disease have been the major causes of the black-footed ferret's decline. The black-footed ferret feeds mostly on prairie dogs that once thrived in its habitat.

Kangaroo rats, *Dipodomys heermanii morroensis*, are rodents that survive only in a small area of Morro Bay in California. Fewer than one hundred of these rats now live surrounded by houses, coastal dunes, swamps, neighborhood cats, automobiles on the roads, low-growing vegetation, and accidental fires. The risks for survival are great for this harmless mammal.

Salt marsh harvest mice, *Reithrodontomys raviventris*, live in salty and murky swamps in the San Francisco Bay area in California. More than 80 percent of their native habitat has been drained and filled for urban development.

The North American gray wolf, *Canis lupus*, also known as the timber wolf, is still stable in densely wooded areas of the northern and western regions of the continent. In 1989, 1,200 were counted in Minnesota, and there may be as many as 30,000 in Canada. However, the numbers in other regions are so small their disappearance seems unavoidable. In 1989, there were no more than 50 in Mexico, 20 in Montana, and 12 in Idaho. Populations in Michigan and

27

Wisconsin may already have been eliminated.

The decline of the red wolf, *Canis rufus*, poses another problem. Its main threat is crossbreeding with coyotes. The wild populations of Texas and Louisiana number only a few dozen wolves of pure stock. Reproduction programs begun in 1977 took fourteen pure stock red wolves into captivity to mate without crossbreeding. In 1989, there were eighty-three pure stock offspring. These pure breeds are slowly being released into the wild with hopes of reestablishing a pure population.

The eastern pumas, *Felis concolor cougar*, also referred to as cougars or mountain lions, live in the United States and Canada. The pumas' presence is linked to that of the wild game, such as deer, that they feed on. Although

▲ The last of the pure red wolves run the risk of disappearing soon.

the pumas' numbers are low, and the animals are protected, cattle ranchers, who consider the pumas a threat, probably still kill them. Destruction of natural habitat presents another threat to the pumas.

Once a species is lost, it is lost forever. No amount of technology can replace the animal. Action must be taken now to save natural habitats and to keep endangered animals safe from hunting and poaching, introduced predators, and pollution.

```
∧∨∧∨∧∨∧∨∧∨∧∨∧∨∧∨∧∨∧∨∧∨∧∨∧∨∧∨∧∨∧∨∧∨∧∨∧∨∧∨∧
```

SCIENTIFIC NAMES OF THE ANIMALS IN THIS BOOK

Animals have different names in every language. To simplify matters, researchers the world over have agreed to use the same scientific names, usually from ancient Greek or Latin, to identify animals. With this in mind, most animals are classified by two names. One is the genus name; the other is the name of the species to which they belong. Additional names indicate further subgroupings. The scientific names for the animals included in *In Peril: Endangered Animals of the Northern Continent*s are:

Algerian tortoise . . . . *Testudo graeca*
American crocodile . . . . *Crocodylus acutus*
Arabian oryx . . . . *Oryx leucoryx*
Asiatic lion . . . . *Panthera leo persica*
Asiatic wild ass . . . . *Equus hemionus khur*
Bali tiger . . . . *Panthera tigris-balica*
Black-footed ferret . . . . *Mustela nigripes*
Black-necked crane . . . . *Grus nigricollis*
Blind salamander . . . . *Typhlomolge rathbuni*
Blunt-nosed lizard . . . . *Gambelia silus*
Cabot's tragopan . . . . *Tragopan caboti*
California condor . . . . . *Gymnogyps californianus*
Central Asian cobra . . . . *Naja naja oxiana*
Chinese alligator . . . . *Alligator sinensis*
Chinese crested tern . . . . . . *Sterna zimmermanni*
Chinese monal pheasant . . . . *Lophophorus lhuysii*
Clapper rail . . . . *Rallus longirostris levipes*
Crocodile of Siam . . . . *Crocodylus siamensis*
Eastern puma . . . . *Felis concolor cougar*
Eld's deer . . . . *Cervus eldi*
Eskimo curlew . . . . *Numenius borealis*
False gavial . . . . *Tomistoma schlegelii*
Giant panda . . . . *Ailuropoda melanoleuca*
Gray's bat . . . . *Myotis grisescens*
Helmeted hornbill . . . . *Rhinoplax vigil*
Hoki . . . . *Crossoptilon mantchuricum*
Houston toad . . . . *Bufo houstonensis*
Imperial woodpecker . . . *Campephilus imperialis*
Indian elephant . . . . . *Elephas maximus maximus*
Indian gavial . . . . *Gavialis gangeticus*
Italian gray partridge . . . . . . *Perdix perdix italica*
Ivory-billed woodpecker . *Campephilus principalis*
Java tiger . . . . *Panthera tigris sondaica*

Javan rhinoceros . . . . *Rhinoceros sondaicus*
Javanese wattled lapwing . . *Vanellus macropterus*
Kangaroo rat . . . *Dipodomys heermanii morroensis*
Komodo dragon . . . . *Varanus komodoensis*
Latifi viper . . . . *Vipera latifii*
Leopard frog . . . . *Rana pipiens fisheri*
Loggerhead turtle . . . . *Caretta caretta*
Long-fingered salamander . . . .
. . . . *Ambystoma macrodactylum croceum*
Mexican desert turtle . . *Gopherus flavomarginatus*
Monkey-eating eagle . . . . . *Pithecophaga jefferyi*
Narrow salamander . . . . *Batrachoseps aridus*
North American gray wolf . . . . *Canis lupus*
Olm . . . . *Proteus anguinis*
Orangutan . . . . *Pongo pygmaeus*
Oriental black ibis . . . . *Pseudibis davisoni*
Persian fallow deer . . . . . *Dama mesopotamica*
Philippine crocodile . . . *Crocodylus mindorensis*
Pond turtle . . . . *Batagur baska*
Prairie dog . . . . *Cynomys parvidens*
Red wolf . . . . *Canis rufus*
Salt marsh harvest mouse . . . .
. . . . *Reithrodontomys raviventris*
San Francisco garter snake . . . .
. . . . *Thamnophis sirtalis tetrataenia*
Snow leopard . . . . *Panthera uncia*
Spotted salamander. . . . . . *Ambystoma maculatum*
Tamarau . . . . *Anoa mindorensis*
Vancouver marmot . . . . *Marmota vancouverensis*
Whooping crane . . . . *Grus americana*
Yak . . . . *Bos grunniens*
Yangtze River dolphin . . . . *Lipotes vexillifer*

GLOSSARY

artificial population — wildlife brought into the world by other than natural means.

birds of prey — carnivorous (meat-eating) hunting birds.

captive breeding programs — the raising of animals in captivity where the resources they need and protection against harm are provided.

captivity — a state of confinement or a controlled environment.

colony — a group of animals or plants, usually with similar characteristics or interests, that lives or grows together.

crossbreeds — when one animal mates with another of a different species.

deforestation — the cutting down or clearing out of trees in a forest.

endangered — in peril or danger of dying out, or becoming extinct.

extinction — the dying out of all members of a plant or animal species.

habitat — the surroundings or environment where plant and animals live and grow.

hibernate — to rest or sleep for a long period of time, as some animals do in winter.

migratory — moving from one habitat to another.

pesticide — a chemical used to kill plant and animal pests.

species — a grouping of animals with the same physical characteristics.

World Wildlife Fund — an international organization devoted to preserving endangered wildlife, plants, and natural habitats.

MORE BOOKS TO READ

The Californian Wildlife Region. V. Brown and G. Lawrence (Naturegraph)

Discovering Birds of Prey. Mike Thomas and Eric Soothill (Watts)

Heroes of Conservation. C. B. Squire (Fleet)

Wildlife of Cactus and Canyon Country. Marjorie Dunmire (Pegasus)

Wildlife of the Northern Rocky Mountains. William Baker (Naturegraph)

VIDEOTAPES

Call or visit your local library or video rental store to see if these videotapes are available for your viewing.

How to Save Planet Earth. (Pro Footage Library: America's Wildlife)

Predators of the Wild. (Time Warner Entertainment)

Wildlife of Alaska. (Pro Footage Library: America's Wildlife)

PLACES TO WRITE

The following organizations work to educate people about animals, promote the protection of animals, and encourage the conservation of their environments. If you write for more information, be sure to state clearly what you want to know.

Greenpeace
1436 U Street NW
P.O. Box 96128
Washington, D.C.
20009

Wildlife Conservation
    International
185th Street and Southern
    Boulevard
Bronx, NY 10460

Canadian Wildlife
    Federation
2740 Queensview Drive
Ottawa, Ontario
K2B 1A2

Conservation Commission
    of the Northern
    Territory
P.O. Box 496
Palmerston
NT 0831, Australia

Canadian Nature
    Federation
One Nicholas Street
Suite 520
Ottawa, Ontario
K1N 7B7

National Audubon
    Society
700 Broadway
New York, NY
10003

ACTIVITIES TO HELP SAVE ENDANGERED SPECIES

1. Write the United States Department of the Interior, Publications Unit, Fish and Wildlife Service, Washington, D.C. 20240, for a list of endangered wildlife. Then write to government officials and express your support for the protection of these animals and their habitat. Also write to government officials to express your support for strengthening the Endangered Species Act.

2. Contact a nature organization in your area. Ask how you can become involved in helping save wildlife.

3. Do not buy wild or exotic animals as pets. Also, do not buy fur, bearskin rugs, ivory, or any other products that endanger animals.

4. Contact a wildlife rehabilitation center in your area and find out what educational programs or activities it offers to the public.

5. Educate your friends about respecting wildlife. Ask them not to participate in acts of carelessness or cruelty that could injure an animal.

6. Spend a day at the zoo. Are any of the animals you see endangered?

INDEX